EDUCATION LIBRARY SERVICE

Browning Way
Woodford Park Industrial Estate
Winsford
Cheshire CW7 2JN

Phone: 01606 592551/557126
Fax: 01606 861412
www.cheshire.gov.uk/els/home.htm

KT-405-361

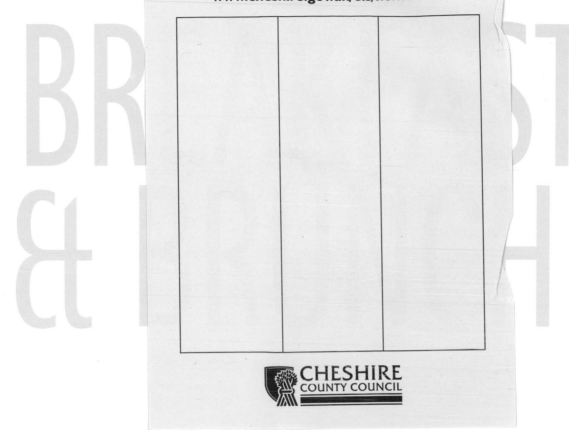

CHESHIRE
COUNTY COUNCIL

Colophon

© 2002 Rebo International b.v., Lisse, The Netherlands

www.rebo-publishers.com - info@rebo-publishers.com

Original recipes and photographs: © R&R Publishing Pty. Ltd.

Design, layout and typesetting: R&R Publishing Pty. Ltd., Victoria, Australia

Cover design: Minkowsky Graphics, Enkhuizen, The Netherlands

ISBN 90 366 1607 7

All rights reserved.

BREAKFAST & BRUNCH

get your day off to a good start with

creative cooking

CHESHIRE
LIBRARIES

1 5 SEP 2004

RL

REBO
PUBLISHERS

Foreword

Inhale a cup of strong black coffee and a cereal bar, then hop in the car for the mad rush to work: sound familiar? This is the usual morning routine for most people. This book proves that you can do things differently. You'll find surprising recipes for your morning appetite.

Traditional dishes, such as scrambled eggs and croissants are included, but you will also find new ideas like Ricotta-Ham Crepes, Cheese and Onion scones, and Champagne Strawberries.

For a large family brunch, you can prepare mouth-watering combinations of rolls, pancakes, and meat.

For those with huge appetites, there are fantastic recipes like Potato Rosti, Wholegrain Pancakes, and even Chili Con Carne. Add a newspaper and a glass of freshly squeezed orange juice and you are sure to start off your day perfectly.

Abbreviations

tbsp = tablespoon	g = gram
tsp = teaspoon	kg = kilogram
oz = ounce	cm = centimeter
lb = pound	ml = mililiter
°F = degrees Fahrenheit	l = liter
°C = degrees Celsius	

Method

Sift flour onto a board, divide into 4. Take ¼ and make a well in the center. Place the yeast in this and mix with about 2-3 tablespoons warm milk and water mixture. The yeast must be dissolved and the dough soft.

Have ready a saucepan of warm water and drop the ball of yeast dough into this and set aside. Add the salt to the rest of the flour, make a well in the center, place in ½ the margarine and work up, adding enough of the milk and water mixture to make a firm paste.

Beat on the board for about 5 minutes. Lift the yeast dough from the water, it should be spongy and well risen, mix into the paste thoroughly. Turn into a floured bowl, cover with a plate, and place in the refrigerator for 12 hours. Roll out the paste to a square, place the rest of the margarine in the center and fold up like a parcel.

Now give the paste 3 turns as for puff pastry, and a fourth if the margarine is not completely absorbed. Rest the paste between every 2 turns and chill before shaping.

When ready for shaping, roll out very thinly to an oblong shape, divide into 2 lengthwise and cut each strip into triangles.

Roll up each one starting from the base and seal tip with beaten egg. Curl to form a crescent, set on a dampened baking tray. Let stand for about 10 minutes then brush with beaten egg. Bake in a hot oven 400°F/200°C for about 25 minutes.

Ingredients

14oz/375g flour

1 tbsp yeast

½ tsp salt

5fl oz/150ml warm milk and water (half and half)

6oz/185g margarine

Croissants

Method

Arrange lettuce, potato salad, tomatoes, egg quarters, olives, tuna, anchovies and French beans in an attractive pattern.

Sprinkle with grated pepper, spoon over the salad dressing, sprinkle all over with parsley and serve immediately.

Note: It is important that this salad does not stand for any length of time.

Mediterranean Vegetable Salad

Ingredients

lettuce, washed and thoroughly dried

1 cup potato salad

4 large tomatoes, peeled and quartered

3 hard-boiled eggs, shelled and cut lengthwise

8oz/220g can tuna in oil, drained and broken into small pieces

4oz/125g black olives

8-12 anchovy fillets, drained

10oz/300g French beans, cooked crisp and chilled

6 tbsp vinaigrette dressing

2$\frac{1}{2}$ tbsp finely chopped parsley

Method

Sift flour with baking powder and salt. Stir in sugar and cornmeal.

Add eggs, milk and melted margarine. Beat until just smooth.

Pour into a 23cm x 23cm x 5cm tin lined with Glad Bake and bake in 220°C oven for 20-25 minutes.

Remove from tin and cut into squares to serve with margarine.

Ingredients

4oz/125g sifted plain flour

4 tsp baking powder

³/₄ tsp salt

1oz/30g sugar

4oz/125g yellow cornmeal

2 eggs

1 cup milk

1oz/30g margarine

margarine, to serve

Corn Bread

Method

Cream margarine and sugar, warm the golden syrup and add. Beat well, then add egg and beat well again.

Sift the flour, ginger and cinnamon, and when thoroughly blended, add the milk in which the soda has been dissolved.

Pour into a 10in/25cm square cake pan and bake in 350°F/180°C oven for 35-40 minutes or until cooked.

Ingredients

4oz/125g sugar

185g margarine

3/4 cup golden syrup

1 egg

9oz/250g plain flour

1 tbsp ground ginger

2 tbsp cinnamon

1 tbsp bicarbonate soda

1 cup milk

Old-Fashioned Gingerbread

Method

Put the couscous and dried cranberries in a bowl. Heat the raspberry and cranberry juice in a pot until it comes to a boil, pour over the couscous and allow to stand for 10 minutes or until all the liquid has been absorbed.

Fold through the strawberries, blueberries, raspberries and mint, if using.

Spoon the couscous into individual bowls and top with a generous dollop of yogurt, sprinkle with the combined seeds and drizzle with maple syrup.

If raspberry and cranberry juice are not available, try apple or pear juice instead.

Ingredients

1 cup couscous

1/2 cup dried cranberries

2 cup/500ml raspberry cranberry juice

7oz/200g strawberries, halved

5oz/150g blueberries

5oz/150g raspberries

1 tbsp chopped fresh mint (optional)

7oz/200g reduced fat vanilla yogurt

2 tbsp sunflower seeds

2 tbsp pepitas

2 tbsp maple syrup

Berry Couscous with Maple Syrup

Method

Line a 7in/18cm pie plate with pastry, keeping back enough for top.

Combine ingredients, place in the pie shell, and cover.

Prick the top, glaze with beaten egg or milk and bake in a

435°F/220°C oven until golden brown. Garnish with parsley.

Ingredients

9oz/250g shortcrust pastry

6 hard-boiled eggs

2 tsp curry powder

1 tbsp mango or tomato chutney

1 cup thick white sauce

1 tsp lemon juice

salt and ground black pepper

1 tsp Worcestershire sauce

Ceylonese Egg Pie

Method

Wash and hull strawberries, sprinkle generously with powdered sugar and place in champagne glasses and chill thoroughly.

Just before serving add chilled champagne.

Champagne Strawberries

Ingredients

1 basket strawberries

1 tbsp powdered sugar

champagne to cover

Method

Place milk, rolled oats, apples, yellow raisins and cinnamon in a saucepan and mix to combine. Cook over a medium heat, stirring, for 5-7 minutes or until oats are soft.

Spoon porridge into serving bowls and serve topped with a spoonful of yogurt.

Fruit and Yogurt Porridge

Ingredients

2 cup/16fl oz/500ml low fat milk

³/₄ cup/2¹/₂oz/75g rolled oats

3 tbsp chopped dried apples

3 tbsp yellow raisins

1 tsp ground cinnamon

2 tbsp low fat natural

fruit yogurt

Method

Preheat oven to 400°F/200°C. Oven temperature is very important to the success of a soufflé.

Grease the bottom and sides of a 8 cup liter soufflé dish with margarine and sprinkle with Gruyére cheese, covering the sides and bottom of the dish.

Melt the 2oz/45g margarine in a medium-sized saucepan over a moderate heat. When foam subsides, stir in the flour with a wooden spoon and stir constantly over a low heat for 1-2 minutes, be sure not to let it brown.

Remove from heat and add the hot milk, stirring well so that the flour and milk are well-blended. Season with salt and pepper and cook over a low heat, stirring constantly, until the mixture comes to a boil and is smooth and thick. Simmer for 1 minute, remove from heat and beat in the egg yolks, one at a time, so that each is blended completely before adding the next one, then add the ham.

Beat the egg whites with a wire whisk until they are so stiff they form peaks. Stir a large spoonful of the egg whites into the sauce to lighten it, then stir in all but a tablespoon of the cheese.

Using a spatula, lightly fold in the rest of the egg whites. Gently pour the mixture into the prepared dish. The dish should be about ³/₄ full. Lightly smooth the surface, and sprinkle cheese on top.

Place the soufflé in the center of the oven and immediately turn the heat down to 375°F/190°C and bake for 25-30 minutes or until well-risen and the top lightly browned.

Ingredients

1 tbsp grated Gruyére cheese

2oz/45g margarine

1oz/30g plain flour

1 cup milk, heated

salt and pepper, to taste

4 egg yolks

6 egg white

1 slice chopped ham

6oz/185g Gruyére cheese

Cheese Soufflé

Method

Just blend all ingredients until smooth.

Breakfast in a Glass

Ingredients

¹/₂ cup honey

1 mashed ripe banana

1 egg

1 cup milk

¹/₂ cup unsweetened pineapple, orange or

grapefruit juice

dash cinnamon

Method

Cut the bacon slices into small pieces and fry until crisp.

Drain on kitchen paper.

Add margarine to pan and cook the mushrooms until soft.

Add salt and pepper.

Just before serving, return bacon to pan and stir in brandy and

cream. Serve with triangles of toast.

Mushrooms and Cream

Ingredients

2 slices bacon

2 tbsp margarine

16oz/500g mushrooms, sliced

salt and pepper

1 tbsp brandy

¼ cup/125ml cream

triangles of toast, for serving

Method

Bring the water and sugar to a boil over a high heat in a fairly large saucepan and stir until the sugar dissolves. Boil briskly for 3 minutes, reduce heat to as low as possible.

Add the peach halves and the vanilla pod and simmer very gently for about 10-20 minutes until they are just tender, be careful not to overcook. Chill the peaches in the syrup.

Heat the raspberries in a heavy saucepan until soft, rub through a fine sieve, using the back of a wooden spoon. Stir in the icing sugar and the lemon juice then the kirsch. Cover the bowl tightly and chill.

Whip cream until it starts to thicken, then sprinkle with powdered sugar and add vanilla. Continue beating until thick enough to hold soft peaks.

Serving: transfer the chilled peach halves to individual serving dishes, use a perforated spoon to do this, so no syrup is served. Coat each peach portion with the sauce, top with cream and decorate with raspberries.

Ingredients

6¼ cups water

16oz/500g sugar

8 large firm ripe peaches, peeled, halved and stoned

1 x 14in piece vanilla pod

Sauce:

16oz/500g fresh raspberries

(keep a few back for garnish)

4oz/125g powdered sugar

juice ½ lemon

1 tsp kirsch

Peaches Cardinal

Cream

150ml thick cream

5 tsp sugar

2-3 drops vanilla essence

Method

Place nectarines, peaches, raspberries and blueberries in a bowl and toss to combine. Divide fruit between serving bowls.

Place yogurt, wheat germ and maple syrup into a bowl and mix to combine. Spoon yogurt mixture over fruit and serve.

Ingredients

3 nectarines, sliced

3 peaches, sliced

4oz/125g raspberries

4oz/125g blueberries

1 cup/6$\frac{1}{2}$oz/200g low fat

vanilla-flavored yogurt

1$\frac{1}{2}$oz/45g wheat germ

1 tbsp maple syrup

Summer Fruit Breakfast

Method

Melt the margarine and cook celery, pepper and onion until tender.

Add the canned soup, milk and cheese and heat until cheese melts, stirring constantly.

Add the eggs, the olives and heat through. Serve over hot toast.

Quick 'n' Easy Eggs à la King

Ingredients

2 tbsp margarine

2oz/60g chopped celery

2oz/60g chopped green pepper

2oz/60g chopped onion

4 hard-boiled eggs, peeled and chopped

1 x 10oz/305g can condensed cream of celery soup

$^1/_2$ cup milk

1 cup diced Cheddar cheese

6 stuffed olives, sliced

hot toast to serve

Method

Cut the cherry tomatoes in half and place on a nonstick baking tray. Grill until soft and the skins begin to shrink. Remove and keep warm.

Put the parsley leaves on another baking tray, lightly spray with the oil and grill until crisp.

Put the egg, egg whites and evaporated milk in a bowl, whisk to combine and season with a little white pepper.

Pour the egg mixture into a nonstick frying pan and cook over a low heat until the egg starts to set. Stir gently until just cooked. Do not overcook otherwise the texture will not be smooth.

Toast the bagels and top the bases with a little of the shaved ham, scrambled eggs, cherry tomatoes and crisp parsley leaves.

Skinny Eggs and Ham on Bagels

Ingredients

3oz/100 g cherry tomatoes

12 leaves parsley

baking spray

4 eggs

¼ cup low fat coffee cream

freshly ground white pepper

2 wholemeal bagels, halved

3oz/100 g low fat ham, sliced

Method

Heat oil in a heavy frying pan. Add bacon and fry until cooked. Place bacon on top of muffin halves; cover and keep warm. Add water to a pan.

Stir in vinegar. Bring mixture to a boil; reduce heat. Break one egg into a shallow dish; slip into water in pan. Repeat with remaining eggs. Simmer, covered, for 3-5 minutes or until eggs are soft-cooked. Remove eggs and place over bacon, cover and keep warm.

Sauce: in a blender, place egg yolks, lemon juice and cayenne. Process until smooth. In a small saucepan, heat butter until melted, but not brown. With the blender running, pour butter into egg mixture in a slow, steady stream. Process a few seconds to thicken the sauce.

Ingredients

6 slices bacon

1 tbsp oil

3 English muffins, split and toasted

6 eggs

paprika

Blender Hollandaise Sauce

6 egg yolks

2 tbsp lemon juice

$1/4$ tsp cayenne

1 cup butter

Eggs Benedict

Method

Cut the bacon into small pieces and fry until crisp. Remove and drain on paper towel.

Add a knob of margarine to the bacon fat and fry the onions until transparent.

Add the potato and keep tossing until golden brown. Return the bacon to the pan, crack in the eggs and stir thoroughly until cooked. Add the parsley and serve piping hot.

Ingredients

1 medium onion, finely chopped

9oz/250g cold mashed potato or cold potatoes diced

1 tbsp finely chopped parsley

4 slices bacon

salt and pepper

knob of margarine

4 eggs

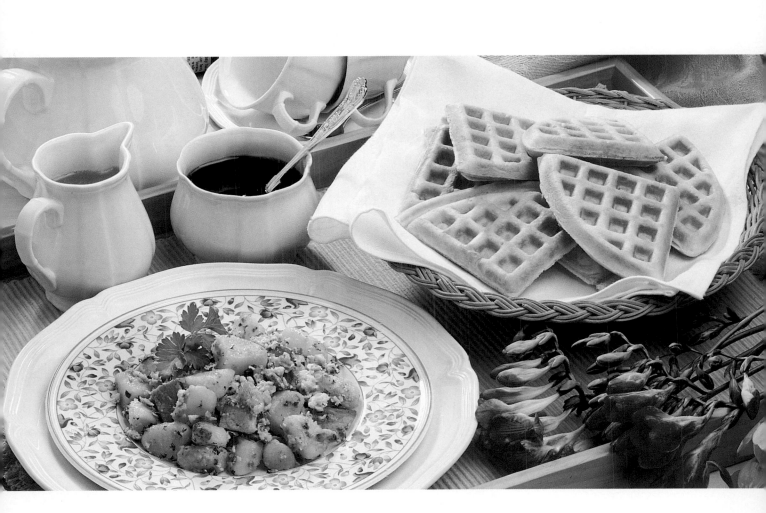

Peasant's Breakfast

briefbreakfast & brunch

39

Method

Grease 2 small ramekins with margarine and place 2 or 3 small slices of cheese in each. Break in the egg, season and add 1 tablespoon cream.

Fill half of the baking dish with boiling, salted water and stand in the ramekins. Water should come nearly to the top.

Cover with a lid or foil and bake gently for about 15-20 minutes or until eggs are set.

Eggs en Cocotte

Ingredients

2 eggs

3 small slices Swiss cheese

salt and pepper

2 tbsp cream

margarine

Method

Boil potatoes for about 4 minutes. Strain and dice. Melt margarine in frying pan, add potatoes and sliced frankfurters.

Keep moving pan, until potatoes are brown. Season and add peas and peppers. Cook for about 5 minutes then add tomatoes and a generous sprinkling of parsley.

Turn the mixture into the bottom of a flat ovenproof dish, break the eggs on top. Season again, pour cream on top and bake in a moderate oven (350°F/180°C) for 6 minutes or until eggs are set. Sprinkle each egg with cayenne pepper before serving.

Ingredients

2 potatoes

60g margarine

2 frankfurts

salt and peppers

2 tbsp cooked peas

2 medium red peppers, cut into shreds

8 tomatoes, skinned, seeded and cut into quarters

4 eggs

parsley

2 tbsp light cream

cayenne peppers

Eggs Flamenco

Method

Sauté the onion and garlic in 1 tablespoon margarine for about 3 minutes or until onion is transparent.

Add chopped chicken livers, cayenne, salt, nutmeg, bay leaf and thyme and continue to sauté for another 3 minutes or until livers have changed color.

Cool, then purée in a blender, or put through fine sieve, gradually working in rest of margarine and lastly the brandy. If not to be used right away, cover with a layer of clarified butter.

Ingredients

1 small onion, chopped finely

1 clove garlic, finely minced

4oz/125g margarine, melted

9oz/250g chicken livers

a pinch cayenne

salt, to taste

a pinch of powdered nutmeg

1 bay leaf

a pinch thyme

1 tbsp brandy

Chicken Liver Paté

Method

Two methods for poaching eggs: first is in an egg poacher. Bring a small amount of water to a boil in the poacher. Grease the cups with margarine, place them in the pan.

Crack the eggs into each cup, cover with the lid and allow just 3 minutes. Easy to remove from liquid with the tip of a thin-bladed knife.

Second method is to use a smallish frying pan, about 10in/25cm. Add just 1in/2.5cm of water to the pan and bring to the boil, then turn down to a gentle simmer. If the water is boiling too fast the egg whites will lose their shape.

Crack the egg into a cup first and gently slide into the simmering water. You may cook more than one at a time but do not overcrowd. Cook for about 3 minutes, according to the consistency desired.

Serve with ham, tomatoes, chives and ground black pepper if desired.

Ingredients

2 eggs

margarine

ham, tomatoes, chives and pepper, for serving

Poached Eggs

breakfast & brunch

47

Method

Soak rolled oats in milk.

Stir in all other ingredients, except extra milk, cream or yogurt.

Leave overnight after stirring well, covered with wrap.

Serve with extra milk, cream or yogurt.

Ingredients

90g rolled oats

1 cup milk

1 tbsp brown sugar

1 fresh apple, chopped

1 tbsp slivered almonds

1 tbsp raisins

1 tbsp yellow raisins

1 tbsp chopped apricots, figs or dates

extra milk, cream or yogurt for serving

Muesli

Method

Place puffed corn, rolled oats, bran cereal, nuts, coconut, cinnamon, apple juice and honey in a bowl and mix well to combine.

Place mixture in a shallow ovenproof dish, spread out evenly and bake, stirring occasionally, for 20-30 minutes or until golden.

Set aside to cool slightly. Add apricots, pears and dates and toss to combine.

Set aside to cool completely. Store in an airtight container.

Puffed Nut Granola

Ingredients

3oz/90g puffed corn

1 cup/3oz/90g rolled oats

1/2 cup/1oz/30g bran cereal

3oz/90g Brazil nuts, roughly chopped

1oz/30g flaked coconut

1 tsp ground cinnamon

1/3 cup/3fl oz/90ml unsweetened apple juice

2 tbsp honey

4oz/125g dried apricots, chopped

4oz/125g dried pears, chopped

3oz/90g cored fresh or dried dates, chopped

Method

Break eggs into a basin and beat well with a fork - not a rotary beater. Add water, salt and pepper.

Heat omelette pan on a medium heat and add margarine. When frothing pour in egg mixture immediately. Leave for about 10-15 seconds then stir slowly with the flat of a fork. Do this once or twice to distribute the eggs then leave for 5 seconds.

Lift up the edge of the omelette to let any raw egg run onto the edge of the pan. Tilt the pan away from you and fold over the omelette to far side, then gently slide onto a hot serving plate. Fillings should be added before the fold over.

Omelettes

Suggested fillings

Two tbsp grated cheese

sliced mushrooms, fried in margarine

finely chopped cold chicken - add salt,

pepper, chives and a little cream

chopped ham

herbs-before pouring mixture into the pan

add a heaping tbsp of finely chopped chives,

parsley, thyme, marjoram etc.

fish-use any cold fish, cooked, finely

chopped with salt, pepper and a little lemon

juice or cream added

Ingredients

4 eggs

1½ tbsp cold water

ground black pepper

1 tbsp margarine

salt

Method

Place sausages in a saucepan the night before, barely cover with water, bring to a boil and simmer for about 3 minutes.

Remove sausages, cool, then remove skins and split lengthwise. Next morning spread with mustard, chutney or relish and sprinkle grated cheese over top. Grill for a few minutes until cheese has melted and sausages are hot.

Ingredients

2lb/1kg beef sausages

mustard, chutney or relish

tasty cheese, grated

Grilled Sausages Piquant

Method

Warm the oil over high heat in a large, heavy fry pan. Add the sausage, garlic and caraway seeds and stir constantly until sausage is lightly browned.

Add the tomatoes, water and black pepper and cook briskly until most of the liquid has evaporated. Add the peppers and simmer partly covered for 10 minutes.

Break the eggs into a bowl, then add to the sausage mixture, stirring constantly. Cook over a low heat and stir with the flat of a fork until the eggs form into soft but firm scrambled eggs.

Serve at once.

Ingredients

1 tbsp olive oil

1lb/500g hot seasoned sausage, such as Spanish chorizo or Italian pepperoni, cut into ½ in/1cm rounds

1 tsp finely chopped garlic

¼ tsp caraway seed (optional)

3 medium firm, ripe tomatoes, peeled and quartered

6 tbsp cold water

2 medium sweet green peppers - remove seeds and ribs and cut into ½ in/10mm strips lengthwise

ground black pepper

6 eggs

Hot Spiced Sausage and Egg

Method

Scrambled eggs can become a gourmet meal with imaginative additives.

The basic scrambled egg is simple to prepare. Beat the eggs lightly and add milk, salt and pepper.

Heat margarine in a pan, add the beaten eggs, stir continuously with a wooden spoon until a creamy texture. Do not have the heat too high.

Suggested additives

chopped chives or parsley and crisp bacon
crumbles

sliced mushrooms, previously fried in
margarine

skin and grill a tomato and chop finely

finely grated orange rind

dice cooked potatoes, fry to a golden brown
and add

soak anchovies in milk, drain, slice and add

Ingredients

2 eggs

2 tbsp milk

salt and pepper

2 tsp margarine

Scrambled Eggs

Method

Combine sausage mince with mixed herbs, Worcestershire sauce, salt and pepper and mix well. Divide into 6 portions.

With wet hands, flatten out 1 portion of mince. Place hard-boiled egg in centre and mould mince around egg to completely and evenly cover. Repeat with remaining hard-boiled eggs.

Place flour, beaten egg and breadcrumbs in 3 separate shallow containers. Coat each ball with flour, dip in egg and coat with breadcrumbs. Refrigerate for 1 hour.

Heat oil in a deep fryer to 350°F/180°C and fry for about 8 minutes. Drain on paper towels. Serve hot or cold.

Scotch Eggs

Ingredients

1lb/500g sausage mince

¼ tsp mixed herbs

2 tsp Worcestershire sauce

salt and pepper, to taste

6 eggs, hard-boiled and shelled

2oz/65g flour

1 egg, beaten

6oz/185g dry breadcrumbs

oil for deep frying

Method

Dissolve gelatin in hot water, then add vinegar and salt. Chill and when slightly thickened beat in the egg until texture is like wh pped cream. Add the gherkins, pepper, olives, pepper, mayonnaise and whipped cream. Lastly add salmon which has bones removed and is broken up finely. Place in a mould and chill firm.

Serve with lettuce and cucumber slices.

Ingredients

13oz/375g canned red salmon	salt and pepper, to taste
1 tbsp fine chopped green capsicum	4oz/125ml mayonnaise
5 tsp gelatin	2 sweet gherkins, chopped finely
1³/₄ cups hot water or fish stock	4 black olives, cored and chopped
2 tbsp wine vinegar	4oz/125ml whipped cream
	1 egg

Salmon Mousse

63

Method

Remove membranes from kidney and cut into small pieces. Chop the bacon finely and fry until fat is transparent. Drain on kitchen paper.

Add 1 tablespoon Flora Sunflower Oil to bacon fat and sauté the onion and celery until onion is transparent. Remove and drain on kitchen paper.

Dust the kidney pieces with flour, add the remaining tablespoon of oil to the pan and sauté kidneys until they change colour, tossing gently all the time.

Return the bacon, onion and celery to the pan, add salt and cayenne, bay leaf, mace, tomato paste, stock and sherry, cover pan with lid and cook gently for about 25-30 minutes. Serve on hot toast spread with margarine and garnish with parsley.

Ingredients

1 medium-sized ox kidney	salt to taste
3 slices bacon	1 bay leaf
2 tbsp Sunflower oil	pinch nutmeg or mace
1 small onion, finely chopped	1 tbsp tomato paste
large stick celery or 2 small, chopped finely	1 cup chicken stock
2oz/65g plain flour	2 tbsp sweet sherry
¼ tsp cayenne pepper	hot toast, to serve
	margarine, for toast

Kidney Creole

Method

Wash and trim scallops and dry carefully.

Butter a baking dish, place in the scallops, dot with margarine and season to taste with salt and ground pepper. Place under the griller about 3in/7.5cm from the heat and grill until golden brown.

This should take about 5 minutes.

Sprinkle with lemon juice and garnish with parsley.

Ingredients

1lb/500g scallops, shucked

2 tbsp margarine

salt and pepper

lemon slices, to serve

parsley, to garnish

Grilled Scallops

Method

Melt margarine in saucepan, add flour and stir until smooth.
Add stock, bring to a boil, stirring constantly. Remove from heat,
add the meat and seasonings and lastly the cream. Turn onto a plate
to cool.

Mold into small cork shapes when cool, roll in flour, then in beaten
egg and lastly breadcrumbs. Melt an equal quanity of margarine and
oil in a pan, heat and fry croquettes to a golden brown.

These could be prepared overnight and fried in the morning.

Ingredients

30g margarine

1 tbsp plain flour

1/3 cup chicken stock

6oz/185g cooked chicken, finely chopped

2oz/60g chopped ham

salt and pepper

1 tbsp cream

plain flour, egg and breadcrumbs, for coating

margarine and oil, for frying

Chicken Croquettes

Method

Place kippers into a pan, cover with boiling water and simmer for 5 minutes.

Remove kippers from pan, drain well, dot with margarine and place under griller for 2-3 minutes.

Serve with lemon and extra margarine.

Kippers

Ingredients

2 kippers

1 tbsp margarine

lemon wedges, to serve

extra margarine, to serve

Method

Combine chili sauce, mustard, milk, blue cheese, minced steak, sausage mince, sage, breadcrumbs and eggs in a bowl. Mix well and press into a greased loaf tin. Bake at 375°F/190°C in oven for 1¼ hours.

Heat margarine in a saucepan, cook onion and capsicum until soft. Add extra chili sauce and water and cook until thickened.

Spread onion mixture over meat loaf and continue baking for additional 15 minutes. Turn out and serve hot or cold.

Ingredients

60ml chili sauce

½ tsp mustard

1 cup milk

4oz/100g crumbled blue cheese

1½ lb/750g minced steak

4oz/125g sausage mince

¼ tsp sage

2 cup fine white fresh breadcrumbs

2 eggs, beaten

2 tbsp margarine

1 onion, finely chopped

2oz/60g finely chopped green capsicumpepper

2fl oz/60ml chili sauce, extra

2 tbsp water

Meat Loaf Supreme

Method

Mix first 5 ingredients until very smooth then add water and continue beating until consistency of thin cream.

Refrigerate for at least 2 hours before using. Heat a little oil in a 15cm frying pan and make crepes one by one, adding a little more Flora Sunflower Oil for each one and using about 2 tablespoons batter.

Combine filling ingredients. Place 2 tablespoons of filling into each crepe, roll up and place side by side in a well-greased heatproof dish. Dot with margarine, sprinkle with parmesan cheese and bake in a 400°F/200°C oven until lightly browned. Serve with salad.

Ricotta and Ham Crepes

Ingredients

Crepes

2 eggs

3/4 tbsp Sunflower oil

1½ tbsp cream

6 tbsp sifted flour

pinch salt

⅓ cup cold water

Filling

4oz/100g ricotta cheese

4 tbsp chopped, cooked ham

salt and freshly ground pepper

margarine

Method

Place the cod in a pan, cover with water and the juice of ½ lemon. Bring to boil, simmer for 5-6 minutes, until heated through. Drain, remove bones and flake.

Place drained cod into a saucepan with cream, juice of remaining ½ lemon, pepper and parsley. Heat through and serve on toast triangles, spread with margarine.

Creamy Smoked Cod

Ingredients

2lb/1kg smoked cod

1 lemon

10fl oz/300ml cream

ground black pepper

2 tbsp chopped parsley

toast triangles, to serve

margarine

Method

Combine the first 7 ingredients. Form into balls and sauté in the hot Sunflower oil until browned.

To make the sauce: combine all sauce ingredients. Bring to boil, simmer 5 minutes.

Add the meatballs. Simmer covered for 20 minutes over a low heat. Uncover and cook for 10 minutes longer.

Ingredients

1lb/500g minced topside

2oz/45g brown rice

1 onion, chopped

1 clove garlic, finely chopped

½ tsp salt

1 egg

1 tbsp chopped parsley

4 tbsp Sunflower oil

Sauce

1 cup tomato sauce

¼ cup vinegar

3 tbsp brown sugar

1 green pepper, chopped

Sweet and Sour Meatballs

Method

Sift the flour, baking powder and salt together, then rub in the margarine. Beat the eggs and milk together and add to flour mixture to make a firm dough.

Add finely mashed potatoes, shallots and pepper. Stir through lightly. Turn onto a floured board, or sheet of nonstick Glad Bake, knead, then roll out to very small thickness. Cut into rounds and bake in 450°F/230°C oven for 30 minutes. Split open while hot and spread with margarine and serve.

Ingredients

6oz/185g plain flour

1 tsp baking powder

$\frac{1}{2}$ tsp salt

$\frac{1}{2}$ cup margarine

2 eggs, beaten

$\frac{3}{8}$ cup milk

4oz/125g cold mashed potato

3 shallots, finely chopped

ground black pepper

flour, for kneading

margarine, for spreading

Potato Scones

Method

Cook potatoes in their jackets, in boiling salt water until about half cooked (15-20 minutes). When cool enough to handle, slip off skins.

Shred potatoes coarsely into a bowl and m x lightly with onion, salt and pepper.

In a heavy-based, non-stick, medium fry pan, melt margarine and half Flora Sunflower Oil over medium heat. Add potatoes, pressing down with a spatula. Cook over low heat until potatoes are brown and crusty on the bottom, about 10-15 minutes.

Loosen edges with a spatula. Cover pan with a plate, turn potatoes upside down onto it and add remaining tab espoon Flora Sunflower Oil to pan. Swirl to coat pan well. Slide potatoes back into pan and cook until bottom is well browned and crusty, about 10-15 minutes.

Serve from pan or turn upside down onto a warm serving plate.

Ingredients

5 medium potatoes (about 2lb/1kg)

2oz/60g finely chopped onion

½ tsp salt

pinch of pepper

2 tbsp margarine

2 tbsp Sunflower oil

Hash Brown Potatoes

breakfast & brunch

Method

Cook the steak, onions and peppers In a heavy frying pan in Sunflower oil until meat is lightly browned. Stir in the remaining ingredients.

Cover and cook gently for 1 hour.

Ingredients

1lb/500g minced steak

1 cup finely chopped onion

3oz/90g finely chopped green peppers

Sunflower oil, for frying

24oz/810g can tomatoes

13oz/375g can kidney beans, drained

1 cup tomato purée

1 tbsp tomato paste

1 tsp salt

1 clove garlic, minced

1½ tsp chili powder

1 bay leaf

Chili Con Carne

Method

Sift flour, salt and cayenne. Rub margarine into flour. Add grated cheese, parsley and onion and mix well.

Make a well in the center and add beaten egg and milk all at once, and mix quickly to a soft dough. Turn out on a floured board and knead just enough to make a smooth surface.

Roll to ½ in/1cm thickness and cut into rounds. Place on a floured tray, glaze tops with milk or beaten egg and milk. Bake in a hot oven 450°F/230°C for 10-15 minutes or until scones are browned.

Ingredients

1lb/500g self-raising flour

1 level tsp salt

¼ tsp cayenne pepper

2oz/60g margarine

4oz/100g grated cheese

1 tbsp finely chopped parsley

1 level dessert spoon finely chopped onion

1 egg, beaten

1½ cups milk

Cheese and Onion Scones

Method

Make a well in the center of the flour. Combine egg and half the milk together. Pour into the well and gradually blend in the flour to make a thick batter.

Beat thoroughly until smooth, gradually adding rest of milk. Allow to stand for at least ½ hour. (Can be made overnight.)

Allow half a slices of bacon for each pancake. Fry half the bacon slices until nearly crisp then pour enough of the batter around it to make a full-sized pancake. Cook until crisp, turn carefully and cook on reverse side.

Bacon Pancakes

Ingredients

4oz/125g plain flour, sifted

1 beaten egg

1 cup milk

2 slices bacon, rind removed

Method

Sift flour, baking powder, sugar and salt into a bowl, make a well in the center. Add eggs, milk and margarine to the well. Gradually beat in liquid until smooth. Cover and set aside for 10-15 minutes.

Heat pan, brush with a little margarine and pour in ¼ cup pancake mixture. Cook until golden brown, turn and cook other side. Repeat with remaining mixture. Serve warm with extra margarine and maple syrup.

Pancakes

Ingredients

6oz/185g self raising flour

1 tsp baking powder

2 tbsp powdered sugar

pinch salt

2 eggs, lightly beaten

1 cup milk

1 tbsp margarine, melted

extra margarine for brushing

extra margarine for serving

maple syrup for serving

Method

Brush pie plate with melted margarine and smooth on 1 layer of pastry, brush with melted margarine again. Repeat this 8 times, finishing with a topping of melted margarine. Trim edges.

Cook the shallots gently in the 1oz/30g margarine until transparent. Add the spinach and stir over a moderate heat until moisture has evaporated. Add salt, pepper and nutmeg.

Beat eggs and cream and gradually stir in the spinach mixture. Pour into pastry shell, sprinkle with cheese, dot with margarine and bake in 350°F/180°C oven for 25-30 minutes until set and golden.

Filling

2 tbsp finely chopped shallots

30g margarine

1 bunch chopped English spinach

pepper, to taste

pinch nutmeg

15g margarine, cut into tiny dobs

$\frac{1}{2}$ oz/300g cream

11oz/30g grated Swiss cheese

3 eggs

$\frac{1}{2}$ tsp salt

Ingredients

8 sheets filo pastry

2oz/60g margarine, melted for brushing

Spinach Tart

Method

Place flour and sugar in a bowl and mix to combine. Add yogurt, milk and egg and whisk to combine. Fold in blueberries and nuts.

Heat a nonstick frying pan over a low heat, pour 2 tablespoons of batter into pan and cook for 2 minutes or until bubbles appear on the surface. Turn pancake over and cook for 2 minutes longer or until golden on second side. Remove pancake from pan and repeat with remaining batter.

Ingredients

1 cup/5oz/155g wholegrain

self-raising flour

1/2 cup/3oz/90g brown sugar

8oz/250g low fat natural yogurt

1/3 cup/3fl oz/90ml low fat milk

1 egg, lightly beaten

8oz/250g blueberries

3oz/90g macadamia nuts,

roughly chopped

Wholegrain Nutty Pancakes

Index